When I was a teenager, my mother and I visited the Top End. The Northern Territory is a vast area. It is six times the size of Victoria. The Top End is so big that it has different climates. It has tropical rainforests in the northern half and semi-arid desert country towards the south. The top half is the Top End. The south is the Red Centre.

Darwin
Cape York
Wyndham
Derby
Cooktown
Cairns
Tennant Creek
Townsville
Mackay
Alice Springs
Bundaberg
Brisbane
Gold Coast
Geraldton
Kalgoorlie
Perth
Fremantle
Port Augusta
Newcastle
Adelaide
Sydney
Woolongong
Canberra
AUSTRALIAN
CAPITAL
TERRITORY
Albany
Geelong
Traralgon
Hobart

The Aboriginal people in the Top End have been there for thousands of years. Some of the people speak their Aboriginal language every day. They live off the land. Aboriginal culture is strong. The coastal Aboriginal people had contact with people from Indonesia long before Europeans got to Australia. They would trade and share things like weapons, pearls, food, sea slugs and turtle shells. The Top End is where the didgeridoo is used. They call the didgeridoo a yidaki.

Darwin is a large city on the coast with big tide changes. During low tide, the waterline is a long way from the shore. The low tide exposes muddy flats. Around the Darwin area, the Aboriginal people hunt dugong. The dugongs can be three metres long and weigh 400 kilograms. The dugongs come to the surface to breathe through nostrils near the top of their snouts. Dugongs are protected, and only Aboriginal people can hunt them. Native Title is a special law for Aboriginal people which allows them to continue their ancestors' culture. Hunting dugong is part of the First Peoples' culture.

From Darwin, we went on a guided outback safari tour to Kakadu National Park. We travelled in a big 'off-road' vehicle. It was crammed with lots of people from different countries, like Germany, England and America. We all got to know each other on the long drive. It was a very bumpy road. We drove through rivers and muddy tracks to get to the campground.

m
2
1

The next day we set off on a bushwalking, kayaking and swimming adventure. There were high rock cliffs and waterholes. Someone spotted a small crocodile. It was only a baby but I was still scared. The guide told us there are no big crocs because they have been caught and moved. Later, we got to a waterhole. We walked along the trail to a big waterfall. It had clear water and no crocodiles. The waterfall looked terrific, and people went swimming. I still looked out for crocodiles, just in case!

The next day we went on a boat. We went cruising along a big river to see crocodiles. This time we saw large adult crocs. There were buffalo on the banks of the river. There were wild boars and magpie geese. The guide told us that the local Aboriginal people like to eat these. In the Top End, they have many animals. Some are only found in the Top End. I was excited to see many animals in the wild. I saw a group of crocodiles eating a buffalo. It was something I will never forget. The crocodiles are very fierce reptiles.

When I was older, I went to the Red Centre. I went to Uluru near Alice Springs. Uluru is within an Aboriginal National Park. The land belongs to a group of families. Their relatives have lived in this area for thousands of years. They are desert people called Anangu. They can survive in hot and dry places. Some people hunt and gather. The First Nations' People find lizards, seeds, grubs and water. The community all play a part in providing for each other.

I walked around the rim of Uluru. I wanted to look all around it. While walking around, I looked at rock art. Rock art is how the Anangu communicated and shared their knowledge. The rock surfaces are like a classroom board and the Anangu artists are like teachers. This art could be over 30,000 years old.

From Uluru, I went to Kings Canyon. This is home to the Luritja peoples. Kings Canyon has a walking track around the rim. We walked the trail and saw many trees, plants and waterholes. The views inside the canyon and of the desert, were amazing. I liked the feeling of being in the Outback. I liked that this land has many Aboriginal people taking care of it. There were Aboriginal people working as guides at Uluru and Kings Canyon. The land looks ancient with all the red rock and cliffs. It reminds me of just how strong Aboriginal people are to live in these areas.

Our Aboriginal guide took us to his family property. He showed us a large boulder that had grooves. The people long ago would sharpen their spears in this rock. This sharpening process created the grooves. We climbed a high, desert hill and found shells and fossils. Scientists say that before people came to this land, there was a large inland sea. It covered much of the area that is now desert. I was surprised to know this. I was surprised to find shells and fish fossils all over the ground.

On our last day, we had a long drive to Alice Springs airport. On the way, we saw herds of camels. There are thousands of camels in the Red Centre. They were brought here by Europeans. They used the camels to explore the desert areas. They are better than horses in the desert. Today, there are too many camels. Many feral camels cause problems. They sometimes break fences, eat the crops and drink all the water on the farms. They can make it hard for native animals to survive. Even though they cause problems, I did find them interesting. I loved my trip to the Top End!

Word bank

Northern Territory
Victoria
tropical
rainforests
Aboriginal
thousands
language
culture
Indonesia
Europeans
didgeridoo
yidaki
Darwin
dugong
kilograms
nostrils
protected
ancestors
safari
Kakadu
vehicle
Germany
England
America
adventure
bushwalking
kayaking
crocodile
terrific
cruising
buffalo
magpie
excited
fierce
reptiles
Uluru
relatives
Anangu
communicated
knowledge
Luritja
ancient
process
fossils
scientists
cherish